Letts

GRAPHICS MASTER

David Sadler

Letts Educational
Chiswick Centre
414 Chiswick High Road
London W4 5TF
Tel: 020 8996 3333
Fax: 020 8996 8390

First published 2004

Commissioned by Cassandra Birmingham

Editorial, cover and inside design and project
management by DP Press Ltd., Kent.

British Library Cataloguing in Publication
Data. A CIP record of this book is available
from the British Library.

ISBN 1843153300

Letts Educational is a division of Granada
Learning, part of Granada plc.

Acknowledgements
The author and publisher are grateful to the
copyright holders for permission to use quoted
materials and images.
Screen shots reprinted by permission from
Microsoft Corporation.
Every effort has been made to obtain
permission for the use of copyright material.
The author and publisher will gladly receive
information enabling them to rectify any error
or omission in subsequent editions..

Printed in Italy

CONTENTS

0100101010110100101010010101110100101010101011101010101101110000101011

SKILLS

.: Saving work :.

It is important to be able to save your work so that you can come back to it and adapt it later. Your work will be saved as a file and to find it easily it is best to put this file into a folder with similar files. On most computers, these folders will be located in the **My Documents** folder. The first time you save a file you should give it a name. Choose a suitable name and be sure that you know where you are saving it.

When saving an image you should also consider the file size of the image and what you want to do with it. A bitmap image will become blurred if you increase the size or zoom in. It also takes up a lot of memory. If you are going to email the image, then you need to keep the file size as small as possible.

A jpeg file takes up less memory than some other formats. Some programs have their own file types, e.g. Adobe Photoshop saves files as psd files. This is fine, but the person you are sending the program to needs to have the same software as you.

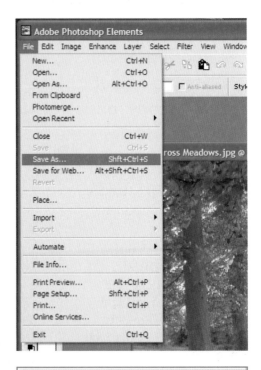

.: Saving work :.

If you have saved the work, you need to know how to open it again when you want to use it in the future.

PC MASTER TIP

If you are not sure what format to use for an image, save it in two or three different formats and compare the quality and file sizes before you use the image.

1001001010110100101001011101001010101011101010110111000010101

 SKILL IN ACTION

Sue the Scientist regularly saves her drawings of apparatus on a computer so that she can adapt them for different experiments. She thinks that the work looks much more professional when she does it on a computer. That is because all the drawings look similar, are the same size and have a similar style.

To adapt this drawing for another experiment, she opens the first image and changes it before saving it with a different file name. (Otherwise, it will replace the first image.)

This is very useful for Sue because it means that she has all her diagrams saved in a folder on the computer so that she does not have to redraw them.

The image below shows a folder with diagrams saved in it.

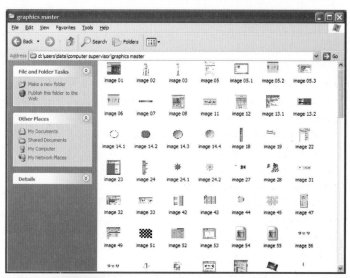

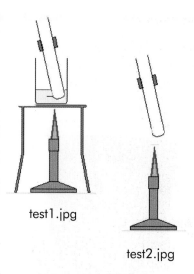

test1.jpg

test2.jpg

EXERCISE

Can you save a file called apparatus.doc?

SKILLS

.: How to save your work :.

When saving your work for the first time, check that it has a sensible name. The computer will guess that you want to call it 'image1' (or something similar) but this is usually not appropriate. You will want to call it something that will remind you of the image. So, you need to use the **Save As** function. Click on **File** then **Save As**, as shown below.

File	Edit	View	Image	Colors	Help
New					Ctrl+N
Open...					Ctrl+O
Save					Ctrl+S
Save As...					
From Scanner or Camera...					
Print Preview					
Page Setup...					
Print...					Ctrl+P
Send...					
Set As Background (Tiled)					
Set As Background (Centered)					
Recent File					
Exit					Alt+F4

.: How to open your work :.

There are two ways to open your work. If you find the file in a folder, you can double click on it and the computer will guess which program you want to use. You can usually see this by the icon next to the file name.

If this does not work (a jpeg file can be opened by many different applications), open the required application first, then click on the **Open** icon or click on **File**, then **Open**. You should then be able to locate the file and open it.

Open icon

.: Saving options :.

If you want to save the file after opening it, unless you want to rename the file, you can just press the **Save** icon on the **File** menu.

If you do not want to write over the old image, change the file name by saving the image using **Save As**.

 PC MASTER TIP

Always save a file with an appropriate name so that you can find it quickly.

1001001010110100101001011101001010101011101010110111000010101

 PROGRESS CHECK EXERCISE

Can you save a document with a new name?

Save an image as a file called 'coursework draft 1'. Click on **Save As** and rename the document by typing the name in the bottom of the menu box that appears.

Can you save a document in a folder?

Find a folder to save your work in. When you have finished the work, click on **Save As**.

Use the menu down the side to find the folder that you want.

Double click on it, name your file and save it.

Can you change the file type of the picture so that it takes up as little memory as possible?

Change the image to a jpg file. This is very similar to changing the name of the file. The white box underneath the file name in the **Save As** menu box displays the file type. Click on the arrow to the right of the box. A list of all the suitable file types is shown. Select a jpg file.

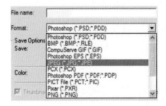

 MASTERCLASS

Can you save a document in a new folder?

HINT: It is always better to save the file in the right place the first time rather than try to move it later. Find the correct folder first, before pressing **Save**. If you want to make a new folder, click on the button shown below.

 New folder icon

Write the name of the folder and then press **Return**. Now you can save the work in the new folder.

CHOOSING COLOURS

SKILLS

.: Colour palettes :.

When creating an image it is important to know how to change the colour produced by the cursor. If you could not do this, you could only produce two colour images, (one for the background and one for the drawing). All the colours are stored on a palette so you need to open the palette to select the colour you want. There are two kinds of palette: the normal palette (shown below) shows a selection of colours to choose from, the other – a custom palette – shows a square of gradually changing colours.

.: A custom palette :.

You can select a precise colour from a custom palette. A custom palette is shown on page 10.

.: Vector drawing colours :.

If you are doing vector drawing, the same principle applies but you can choose a line colour, a text colour and a fill colour separately, so you do not need to (and cannot) colour in with a paintbrush tool.

.: Vector graphics :.

A vector graphic is drawn by using a series of lines. Any drawings created in Microsoft® Office are vector graphics. Vector graphics are a good way of creating images because the computer moves only the start and end points of each line. This uses very little memory and means that images can be enlarged without becoming blurred.

PC MASTER TIP

Once you have the right colour, it can be very hard to match it exactly using a custom palette. It is better to select from the set colours or use the pipette tool to copy the colour from the image.

100100101011010010100101110100101010111010101101110001010101

 ## SKILL IN ACTION

Tammy the Teacher uses different colours to emphasise different labels on a diagram of the water cycle. She wants to show, at each stage of the process, whether the water is a liquid or a gas by using different colours.

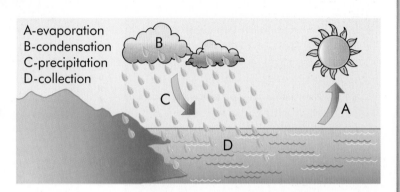

A-evaporation
B-condensation
C-precipitation
D-collection

She also uses this skill to colour in diagrams of the circulatory system to show whether blood is oxygenated or deoxygenated in each part of the body.

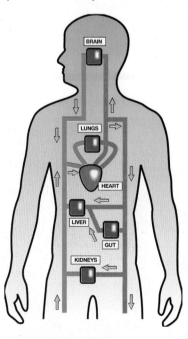

EXERCISE

Can you colour in a black and white image that has either been scanned in from a book or downloaded from the internet? (See page 22.)

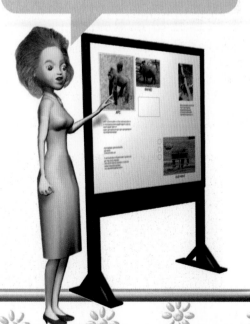

SKILLS

.: Vector graphics :.

Check that the Drawing toolbar is showing. Draw the shape you want then select it. These icons will let you change the colour:

Fill colour   Line colour   Font colour

.: Vector graphics :.

You can change the colour by clicking on the arrows next to the icons. A palette will appear.

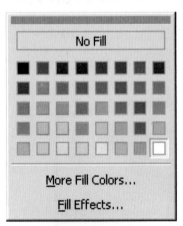

.: Drawing package :.

There is normally an icon to activate the colour palette. The one in Microsoft® Paint is shown below.

.: Drawing package :.

Once the palette is open, click on the required colour or, where possible, choose the custom palette. Click in roughly the right area on the custom palette then use the bar at the side to pick the exact colour. Whatever you draw now will be in this colour.

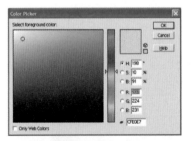

 PC MASTER TIP

The set colours in a palette are often referred to as 'swatches'.

PROGRESS CHECK EXERCISE

Can you colour in a shape drawn with vector graphics?

This circle needs to be coloured in.

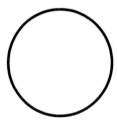

If you press the **fill** icon, it is coloured red.

However, if you do not want a red circle, and want to make it a fading blue colour, use **fill effects** to choose two colours. (See pages 56–59.) Select blue and white and choose how you want it to fade. Then press **OK**. The circle is now filled in as you want.

Can you change the colour of the outline of the shape?

Change the border of the circle to a red colour. On the **line colour** icon click and select red. The image is now as required.

Line colour

Can you change the colour of a paintbrush tool using the custom palette to find an exact colour?

Use Photoshop to create a red circle. Draw a circle first and fill it in. To do this, select the **colour picker** and choose red fading into blue around the edges. Then use the **fill** command to colour it in. (See pages 56–59.) You can then change the colour to blue and use the **airbrush** to spray the edges blue.

 MASTERCLASS

Can you change the colours of a clipart image?

HINT: There are two ways: one is by ungrouping. (See page 32.) The other way is by formatting the image (right click on the image and select **Format Picture**).

0100101010110101010010101010101011010010101010110110101010110110100001010110

SKILLS

.: The toolbar :.

In drawing applications, there are many ways of transferring colour on to an image. The colours are applied by using tools. There is usually a toolbar that shows all the tools that you can use, but you need to try them out to see what they do.

.: Tools :.

The tool that you choose will depend on what you want to do. The main tools are a paintbrush, a pencil and an airbrush. Most packages have some kind of fill tool as well. The lines below are examples of what can be produced by each tool.

Paintbrush

Airbrush

Pencil

Move tool
Marquee tool (select)
Lasso tool
Magic Wand tool (select)
Crop tool
Text tool
Polygon tool
Gradient tool
Airbrush tool
Paintbrush tool
Fill tool
Pencil tool
Erase tool
Art History Brush
Blur tool
Sharpen tool
Sponge tool
Smudge tool
Red eye tool
Dodge tool
Clone tool
Pipette tool
Hand tool
Zoom tool
Colour palette

💡 PC MASTER TIP

The airbrush tool is very useful for taking the sharpness away from an edge. If you look carefully at a photograph, the edges are often slightly blurred. The airbrush tool can give this effect. Select your tools carefully and do not be afraid to use two or three tools on the same area to change the effect.

SKILL IN ACTION

Kate the Kitchen Designer uses many different drawing tools when producing her final designs for customers. As she uses regular shapes, her work looks better if she uses vector graphics. She uses the pencil tool to draw sharp edges, and then she uses the fill tool to colour in the cupboards.

For that final professional look, she copies the picture into Photoshop and uses the airbrush tool to add reflections of light on the cupboards. This adds a 3D effect and makes the paint look glossy.

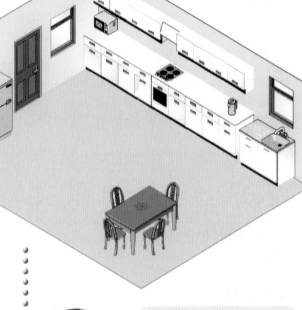

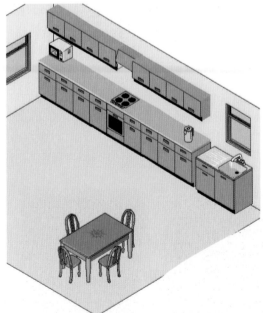

EXERCISE

Can you draw a shape and add texture to it by using a variety of tools?

01001010101101001010010101110100101010101110101010101101011000010101010

SKILLS

.: Selecting a new tool :.

The toolbar is normally open when you start up the drawing package. If it is not, click on the **View** button on the main menu bar. This will have a **Toolbars** option. On this, select the toolbar that you want.

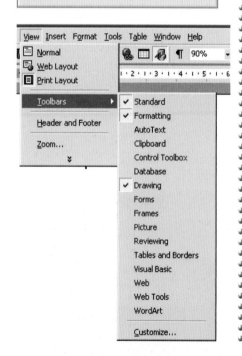

.: New tools in Photoshop :.

To select a new tool in Photoshop, click on **Window** on the menu bar and then select **Show Tools**.

Selection tools

Drawing tools

Modifying tools

Colour tools

.: Photoshop tools :.

These buttons are standard across most applications. The key tools are highlighted.

 PC MASTER TIP

Do not be afraid to try a new tool. Save your work before you try anything though. Then if the effect is not what you are looking for, do not save the amended file, just reopen the saved version.

01001001010110100101001011101001010101011101010110111000010101

PROGRESS CHECK EXERCISE

Can you select the tools needed to draw a star and colour it in?

Select the **line** tool or, if you have autoshapes, look for a star tool there. Draw the star and then use the **fill** tool to colour it in.

Fill tool

To make the star look 3D, use the **airbrush** tool to add a darker colour to the centre of the star and a lighter colour to the edges. This tool can also be used to blur the edges slightly and to give a 'soft focus' feel.

Can you select the tools needed to crop a small detail of a photograph and zoom in to retouch it?

On the photograph below, change the eyes so that they are no longer shiny and crop the cat's head.

Zoom in and retouch the eyes so that they look more realistic and the camera flash is not reflected in them.

 MASTERCLASS

Can you change a photo of someone with red eyes so that they appear the right colour?

SKILLS

.: Zooming in/out :.

To get the best effects, you often need to enlarge an image so that you can work on a small area of it. Then you can use the tools more precisely, to follow guide lines, or to choose your pixels really carefully.

The alterations you make may look obvious while the image is enlarged, but when you go back to normal size, they will be almost invisible.

If you change the size of the image, you might lose some quality. It is therefore better to zoom in and enlarge the image on the screen, without increasing the image size. The memory used by the image will remain the same and the quality will not change.

.: Zoom using vector graphics :.

If you are likely to be working with close-ups, it is better to use vector graphics, as they do not pixelate as you zoom in.

Bitmap image enlarged

Vector image enlarged

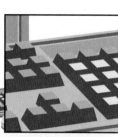

PC MASTER TIP

It is always better to think about what you are going to do with the image before you start making it. Then you can decide what kind of image to produce and will not have to convert it later.

01001000101011010010100100101110100101010101011101010110110000101 0

 SKILL IN ACTION

Ahmed the Artist uses an image creation package to produce some of his art. When he is working in fine detail or needs to make very slight alterations, he zooms in to the area of the image that he is working on. When he has finished, he zooms out.

He scanned in the following image because he wanted to use it in a collage. He decided to remove the buoy by using the clone tool. (See page 88.)

He zoomed in and used the cloning tool to paint over the buoy.

He uses the same process to remove 'red eye' from the photos he has taken.

EXERCISE

Can you zoom in to an area of a piece of art to focus the image on one of the minor characters?

0100101011010010100101011101001010101011101010110111000010101

SKILLS

.: The zoom tool :.

This is a commonly used tool so it has been made very easy to use. Most drawing packages have a zoom tool and a button.

33%

.: Zooming :.

You can also zoom in by using the toolbars. The zoom command is usually found in the **View** drop down menu.

There are usually shortcuts for zooming in and out. In Photoshop, you can hold down **Ctrl** while pressing + or –.

View	Window	Help
New View		
Zoom In	Ctrl++	
Zoom Out	Ctrl+-	
Fit on Screen	Ctrl+0	
Actual Pixels	Alt+Ctrl+0	
Print Size		
Selection Edges		
Show Rulers	Ctrl+R	
Show Grid		
✔ Snap		
Hide Annotations		

.: Zoom tool :.

When you zoom in, you will normally move to the centre of the image. If you want to look at a different area, you need to use the scroll bars to move up and down to find the part of the picture you want.

When you are using vector graphics in an Office application, you normally have to use the zoom tool that zooms in the whole page.

ndow   Help

 ¶ 90%

· 4 · · 5 · · 6 · ·

💡 PC MASTER TIP

It is important to remember to change the brush size or line weight before you zoom in as this does not change automatically. The brush will still draw a line of the same thickness. It will just look thicker if you are zoomed in.

01001001010110100101010010101101001010101101010101101100001010

 PROGRESS CHECK EXERCISE

Can you repair a damaged photographic image?

Choose a photograph from the centre pages of a magazine which has minor damage from the staples and/or the fold or one which has errors caused by light reflections.

Scan the image into a drawing application and use a fine paintbrush to repair it. Zoom in so that you can work precisely.

You can also do this using a clone tool. (See page 88.)

Can you crop an image to see one small detail of it?

You will find it useful to zoom in to see exactly where to crop the image. (See pages 60–63 for more information.)

In a vector diagram, can you zoom in to enable you to carefully cover an unwanted line with a white line?

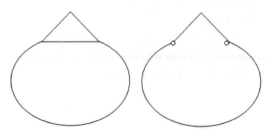

 MASTERCLASS

Can you draw a building with a semi-circular dome using vector graphics?

HINT: Think about covering up unwanted lines with white ones.

01001010101101001010010101110100101010101011101010101101110000101010110

SKILLS

.: Select, copy, paste :.

These three tools are used together and are perhaps the most commonly used tools in any drawing application.

Before you can paste something, you need to copy it and before you copy the image, you need to select exactly what you want to copy.

It can be hard to draw an image precisely. If you can avoid drawing the same thing over and over again by copying it, it will save you time.

.: Clipboard :.

There are a number of ways to copy the selected image. Each method will put the image on a virtual area called the clipboard. You cannot see the image there, but once you paste the image, it will appear where you want it in a document.

.: Paste :.

This can be used in combination with a number of tools to create repetitive patterns or to make an image perfectly symmetrical.

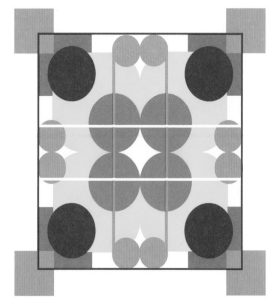

PC MASTER TIP

Sometimes it is better to group the two images produced and copy them so that you can paste lots of copies very quickly.

SKILL IN ACTION

Dave the Designer uses select, copy and paste when he is planning the layout for a classroom. This means he does not have to keep drawing pictures of desks and chairs. Once he is happy with one drawing, he copies it to make sure that all the desks are the same size and shape.

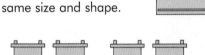

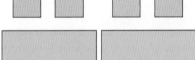

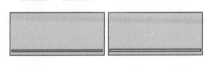

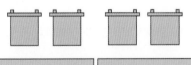

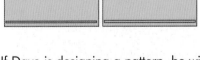

If Dave is designing a pattern, he will use copy and paste to repeat images. This image is drawn using vector graphics in Microsoft® Word.

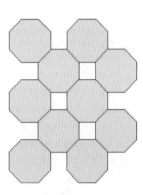

It can be selected, copied and pasted to make a repeating pattern.

Dave also uses copy and paste to repeat a pattern in different places. For example, if he wants the same design in a number of different situations, he can copy and paste it to save drawing it again each time.

EXERCISE

Can you draw a plan view of a desk, then copy and paste it so that there are several identical desks in the room?

SKILLS

.: Selecting an image :.

If you want to use an image from the internet, simply right click on it. The whole image will be selected. (Bear in mind that these images may be subject to copyright laws.)

In a drawing application, use the select tool to select the required area. A dotted line around the selection indicates what will be copied.

In vector graphics, the select tool is slightly different. Click on the **select** tool, click and drag a box over the area required. Dots called 'handles' appear on the selected items.

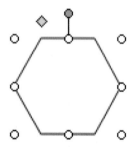

.: Copying an image :.

There are a number of ways of copying an image. On some images, in some applications, you can use a right click and when a menu appears, click on **Copy**. The image is then copied on to the clipboard.

Most applications have a **copy** button which you can click on once an area has been selected. You can also use the menu bar. Click on **Edit** and then on **Copy**.

.: Using a copy shortcut :.

To use a copy shortcut, select the area required. Hold down **Ctrl** while you press the **C** key. The image is then copied on to the clipboard.

.: Pasting an image :.

Pasting the image copies whatever is on the clipboard, and puts it where your cursor is. If you right click on an empty page in Word, a **Paste** option appears. The **Paste** command is also available on the **Edit** drop down menu. The shortcut key for paste is **Ctrl-V**.

PC MASTER TIP

Remember, the image stays on the clipboard until you copy something else or close the application. Once copied, you can paste as many copies as you need or select and move them.

010010010101101001010010101101001010101011101010110111000010101

 # PROGRESS CHECK EXERCISE

Can you draw a chessboard pattern by copying and pasting a black square 32 times?

Can you design a logo to put on a letter, and copy it so that it creates a border around the letter?

Can you draw a plan view of the computer room, or an office, by drawing a desk and computer?

Use vector graphics and then copy and move the objects around the room.

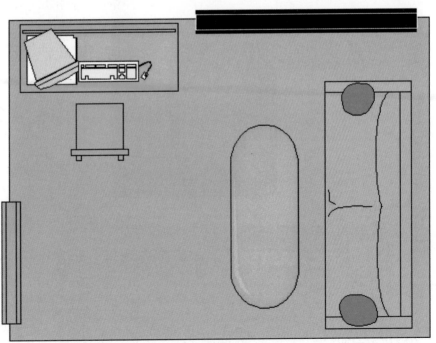

SKILLS

.: Rotate an image :.

If you want to rotate an image to make it upright on the screen, you need to use the rotate tool. It is possible to rotate an image by a set amount, normally 90º clockwise or anticlockwise, or 180º which turns it completely upside down. This is a very useful tool for working with photographs.

Happy
Valentine's
Day

.: Flip clipart :.

It is also useful to flip images, for example, in creating a Valentine card.

The clipart cupids in the top corners are facing the same way. It would give a better feeling of balance if they faced opposite ways. You can do this by using the flip function on the right-hand image.

Happy
Valentine's
Day

PC MASTER TIP

You can use rotate and flip to create an image. Draw a star using vector graphics. Copy and paste it. Then rotate the second image to create a pattern. This can be repeated to form some interesting designs.

010010010101101001010100101011101001010101010101110101010110110100010 10

SKILL IN ACTION

Harry the Hotelier uses the rotate function when he is updating the hotel website. He takes photographs of events at the hotel and different views of the hotel gardens. Some of these photos look better in portrait view and some in landscape. He moves the camera around when he takes the photos to get the best shot, but some appear on their side on his computer. He imports the photos into his software and rotates them clockwise 90º before uploading them on to his website.

landscape

portrait

When Harry produces a menu for a special occasion, he uses clipart around the edge of the menu. He occasionally flips an image to make the menu look more balanced. This often involves copying the image into Photoshop, flipping it and then copying it back into Word.

EXERCISE

Can you create a border for a Valentine's menu by inserting, flipping and rotating images?

SKILLS

.: The rotate tools :.

It is simple to rotate a photograph. Most image applications have a rotate tool that rotates by degrees. First, work out whether you want to turn the image clockwise or anticlockwise. On Windows XP, there are icons that rotate the image at a single click.

 Rotate icon

.: The rotate tools :.

In an image application, select the image then click on **Image** and **Rotate**. There should be options to rotate in every possible way.

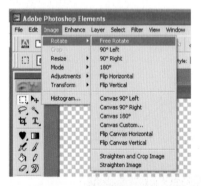

.: The free rotation tool :.

It is also possible to rotate an image by any number of degrees. This is often called free rotation. You can specify the exact number of degrees you want to rotate the image and in which direction.

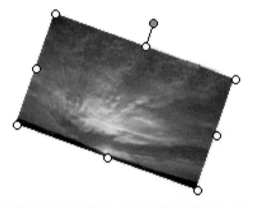

.: The flip tool :.

Flip is used to keep the image the same way up but makes it face in the opposite direction. This can be useful with clipart and drawings but care is needed as writing will read backwards and a face will appear as a mirror image.

PC MASTER TIP

If you start to rotate an object and you find it is the wrong way round, you can either press **Undo** or keep rotating.

01001001010110100101001011101001010101110101011011100001010

 ## PROGRESS CHECK EXERCISE

Can you rotate a photograph so that it spins all the way round?

Can you create a flower in Photoshop by drawing a petal and then copying it, pasting it and rotating it?

First draw the petal.

Then copy and paste it.

Rotate the petals.

Then you can complete the flower with a circle in the middle.

 ## MASTERCLASS

Can you make a pattern by copying a square and rotating it a small amount, repeating this until you get back to the start?

SKILLS

.: Canvas size :.

Canvas size is different from the original image size. The canvas size is the size of the final image you are creating. It may be the same as the size of the original image, but if you decide to add a border to your image, the canvas size will become bigger.

.: Photo collage :.

You might also decide to make a collage of photos. This can be done by making a large canvas size and inserting lots of different images.

PC MASTER TIP

It is better to keep each image in a separate layer so that you can work on it independently from the other images. (See pages 68–71.)

1001001010110100101010010111010010101010110101011011100010101

SKILL IN ACTION

Seema the Stylist changes the canvas size of an image to create a collage of haircut styles for customers to choose from. She likes the idea that a customer can see many different styles on the same piece of paper. She could do this by cutting and pasting photos from magazines and colour photocopying them. But it is cheaper to use her computer to make multiple copies and print them out. It also means that she can change the size of the photos in relation to each other by resizing them. If needed, she can adapt the colours.

This can look very professional and it can be changed from month to month.

EXERCISE

Can you make a collage of photographs and put a border around them by changing the canvas size?

0100101011010010100101110100101010101110101011011100001010110

SKILLS

.: The resize menu :.

Open an image in your graphics application. The image will probably fill the size of the box that it is in. To change the size of the canvas, click on **Image** on the menu bar, then select **Resize**.

.: The canvas menu :.

Click on **Canvas Size** and a further menu appears.

.: Changing the canvas size :.

Type in the proportions that you want the new image to have and then use the **Anchor** menu to let the computer know whereabouts on the new image you want the initial image to appear. You can then either paint in the white areas or add further photos to create a collage.

Canvas Size ☒

Current Size: 285K
Width: 12.49 cm
Height: 9.67 cm

New Size: 285K
Width: 12.49 cm ▾
Height: 9.67 cm ▾
Anchor:

OK
Cancel
Help

 PC MASTER TIP

While changing the canvas size is not difficult, it might be easier to make each image smaller so that they fit onto a smaller canvas. Think of the memory you would save!

0100100101011010010100101110100101010101110101011011100001010

PROGRESS CHECK EXERCISE

Can you create a border for one of your photos?

You will need to increase the canvas size by at least three centimetres in both directions and anchor the image in the middle.

You can then colour in the border to give the effect you want.

This gives a different feel to the photograph when it is displayed in a frame.

Now create a collage. Select five or six photographs from a trip you have made recently. Resize the canvas so that you can fit them all on one image.

 MASTERCLASS

Resize your collage so that it fits perfectly into a picture frame when you print it out.

SKILLS

.: Grouping :.

This skill is only really used with vector graphics. Perhaps the hardest part of vector graphics is drawing irregular shapes. This can be done by layering shapes over one another to cover up the parts of the lines that you do not want to see.

.: Drawing an irregular shape :.

To draw the simple irregular shape below, draw two ovals with black lines and cover up the middle section with a white box or circle. The one image is made from three simple shapes.

.: Moving the image :.

When you want to move the drawing however, each part of the image remains as a separate object. Some parts may move, while others may not. To avoid this problem, you can group the parts. This makes the whole drawing into one object. Then all the parts move together and the shape remains the same.

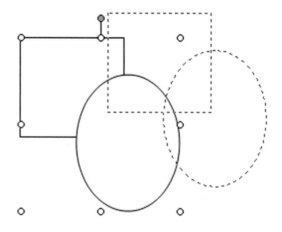

PC MASTER TIP

You have to ungroup objects when you want to change one part of an image. Remember to group them again afterwards!

SKILL IN ACTION

Vicrum the Vet uses grouping when he creates the logo for his practice. He uses a combination of clipart and vector graphics to design the logo and then he uses a text box for the name.

The logo was made using the following clipart:

A text box was added with the practice name in.

To make it easier to copy on to all his documents, he groups the parts to form the logo.

To celebrate ten years of service, he ungroups the logo to change the text.

EXERCISE

Can you design a logo for a vet and group the images to make them easy to copy?

01001010110100101001010110100101010101011101010110111000010101 10

SKILLS

.: Selecting images :.

Care must be taken to select all the parts of an image before grouping them. Click on one part, then holding down the shift key click on all other parts until they have all been selected.

The parts of the image you have selected will have dots over them called 'handles'. If there are any parts without these handles, they may not have been selected and you should make the selection again. It is then just a matter of pressing the **Group** button.

.: Selecting images :.

One easy way is to click on the white arrow on the Drawing toolbar and draw a box over the area to be grouped. It must include all parts of the image. Give yourself a wide border around the outside to make sure that everything is covered.

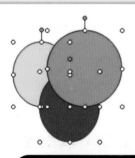

.: Grouping images :.

When you are sure the selection is correct, keep the mouse within the image area and click on **Draw** on the Drawing toolbar and then **Group**.

.: Ungrouping images :.

To ungroup the objects, select the drawing, right click on it and click on **Ungroup**.

If you have grouped a part of the drawing previously, you may need to press ungroup again to make that part also separate into individual bits.

PC MASTER TIP

Once you have grouped some objects and finished the work you can add the image to your clipart.

PROGRESS CHECK EXERCISE

Can you group several objects drawn with vector graphics so that they appear as one object?

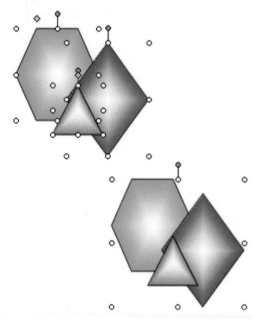

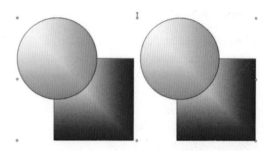

Now copy these two as one object.

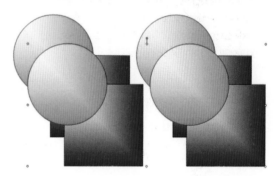

Can you repeat the image by copying and pasting it, then group these two objects before copying and pasting them again to make four?

For example:

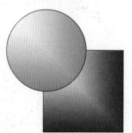

Once you have pasted them, group them again. Copy and paste them to make eight objects.

This is a really quick way of producing many copies of the same image on one page.

MASTERCLASS

Can you ungroup some clipart to change some of the colours and then regroup the parts again?

0100101010110100101010010101110100101010101011101010101101110000101010110

SKILLS

.: Order tool :.

When using vector graphics, the order in which the images appear on the page is very important. Regular shapes are adapted by laying one object on top of another. Each drawing is automatically placed on top of the previous ones. The order tool allows you to change this order so that a particular object can be placed behind or in front of the others.

.: The order tool :.

The circle is supposed to be behind the star but it was drawn after it. It therefore appears on top of the star.

.: The order tool :.

Using the order tool, you can reverse this so the star appears on top.

 PC MASTER TIP

There is a real art to drawing objects in vector graphics. You need to think about how to cover up unwanted parts, when and where to group objects and how to order them so that whatever is actually drawn, the only visible parts are those you want to be seen.

SKILL IN ACTION

Dave the Designer uses the order tool to design company logos. He decides to use vector graphics to make the logos because they often need to be resized for various purposes. If they are going to be much bigger, e.g. on vehicles or office doors, then they will need to be enlarged without blurring. Using vector graphics to draw the image will avoid it become pixelated. Dave needs to layer the objects in the correct order. Otherwise, some will be hidden.

The logo below shows a star beneath a red circle. Dave wants the star to be on top.

By using the order tool, he can bring the star to the front.

The logo is now taking shape. Dave needs to make sure that the text is on top of the image so that the name on the finished logo is visible.

EXERCISE

Can you design a logo and change the order of the objects so that the logo looks completely different?

0100101011010010100101110100101010101110101010110111000010101010

SKILLS

.: The Order menu :.

Changing the order of images is very easy. The hard part is making sure that the order is correct. There are a number of options in the Draw menu on the Drawing toolbar. Click on **Draw**, select **Order** and another menu appears.

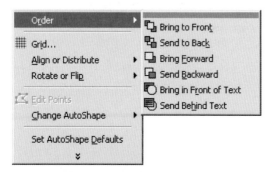

Order ▶	
▦ Grid...	🔲 Bring to Front
Align or Distribute ▶	🔲 Send to Back
Rotate or Flip ▶	🔲 Bring Forward
✏ Edit Points	🔲 Send Backward
Change AutoShape ▶	🔲 Bring in Front of Text
Set AutoShape Defaults	🔲 Send Behind Text
⌄	

.: Using the Order menu :.

To correct this, click on the front table leg and use the **Bring Forward** option. This moves it back a layer and the chair appears to be tucked under the table.

.: Using the Order menu :.

The options on the Order menu are self-explanatory. You can send the object back a layer, bring it forward a layer, move it to the front or to the back.

This drawing of a table and chairs was done in a vector drawing program called AspexDraw. The chairs are over the table. They need to be behind it.

💡 PC MASTER TIP

The order the objects appear in depends on the order in which they were drawn. The first object drawn will always be behind the second unless you change the order.

1100100101011010010100101011101001010101011101010110111000010101

 ## PROGRESS CHECK EXERCISE

Draw a text box in Word with some writing in it.

Can you draw another box over the top and send it to the back?

To do this you will need to have the Drawing toolbar open. If it is not, click on **View**, then **Toolbars**. The following menu appears:

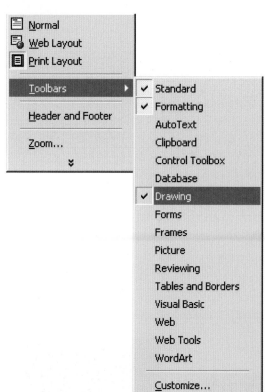

Click on the **Drawing** option and the toolbar will appear at the bottom of the screen.

Draw a second, larger box over the first and colour it red.

Now select the object that you want to send to the back: in this case, the red box.

Select **Draw**, then **Order** and another menu will appear.

Choose **Send to Back** and the object moves behind the text box to give a border effect.

This will only appear with the red box at the back

 ## MASTERCLASS

Can you draw five objects on top of each other getting progressively larger, then change the order so that they appear progressively smaller?

01001010110100010100010101110100010101010111010101011011011000010101 0

SKILLS

.: **Edit points** :. ⬍

When you are drawing a shape with vector graphics, the end of a line may not go exactly where you want it to. The edit points tool allows you to move each end of the line by minute amounts so that you can place the line in exactly the right place. This is especially useful when covering up part of an image.

.: **Edit points** :. ⬍

This shape is created using vector graphics but there is part of a black line showing. You can cover this up by drawing a white box over it.

.: **Edit points** :. ⬍

The white box has not completely covered these parts of the shape. By using the edit points tool you can cover it exactly.

💡 PC MASTER TIP

This is a very useful tool if you are labelling points on a diagram as you can point the line to exactly where you want it to go.

110100101010110100101010010110100101010101101010101101110000101 01

SKILL IN ACTION

Kate the Kitchen Designer uses edit points to make sure that her kitchen units fit together perfectly. In the drawing below, the kitchen surfaces do not meet up exactly. This is not acceptable and does not look as professional as it might. It would certainly be unacceptable if the kitchen was actually constructed in this way. Therefore to get the best idea of what the room will look like, the drawing needs to look perfect.

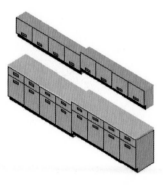

Using edit points, Kate can move the ends of the lines by very small amounts so that they meet up exactly.

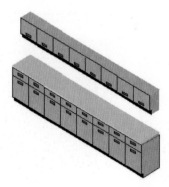

This makes her work look more professional and could result in her company receiving a contract over another one.

EXERCISE

Can you draw a cooker in 3D using vector graphics? You will need to use edit points to make sure that all the knobs are in the correct place.

01001010110100101001011101001010101110101011011000010101

SKILLS

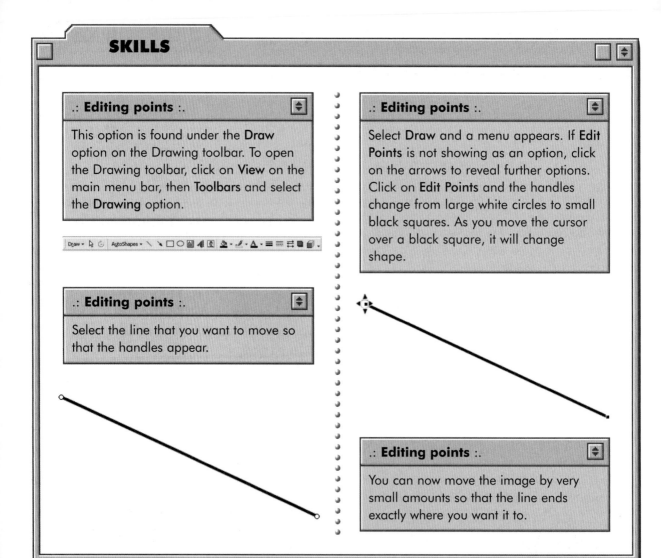

.: Editing points :.

This option is found under the **Draw** option on the Drawing toolbar. To open the Drawing toolbar, click on **View** on the main menu bar, then **Toolbars** and select the **Drawing** option.

.: Editing points :.

Select the line that you want to move so that the handles appear.

.: Editing points :.

Select **Draw** and a menu appears. If **Edit Points** is not showing as an option, click on the arrows to reveal further options. Click on **Edit Points** and the handles change from large white circles to small black squares. As you move the cursor over a black square, it will change shape.

.: Editing points :.

You can now move the image by very small amounts so that the line ends exactly where you want it to.

PC MASTER TIP

Some vector drawing programs have a grid. Sometimes there is an option called **Snap to Grid** (or something similar) which means that each line can only begin or end at a set point. All lines will meet up at these points and therefore there is less of a need to use edit points.

0100100101011010010101001011101001010101011101010110111100001010

 PROGRESS CHECK EXERCISE

Can you label a diagram precisely so that the arrows point exactly to each object?

If the label line will not reach the required place exactly, you can use edit points to move it. The line below needs to be moved slightly higher to label the part.

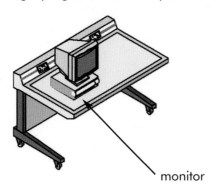

monitor

Select **Edit Points** and move the line the small amount required.

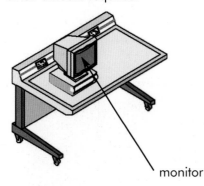

monitor

Can you cover up the unwanted part of an image with a white line so precisely that none of the unwanted black lines appear?

Draw the white line over the shape first and make the line thicker using the **line style** button on the Drawing toolbar. This should cover most of the unwanted part.

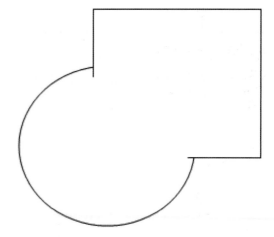

Use edit points to move the thick, white line to exactly cover the rest of the unwanted area.

 MASTERCLASS

Can you draw a diagram of the human eye using vector graphics? Use the order and grouping tools to cover up all the unwanted lines.

SKILLS

.: Autoshapes :.

Autoshapes are custom shapes that are drawn automatically by the computer. There are many shapes to choose from, including all the geometric shapes, stars or smiley faces. These shapes can be adapted to show various angles of slope, any number of points or different faces. Autoshapes can be filled in in the same way as regular shapes, so they are very useful as it can be hard to colour in shapes using vector graphics.

Autoshapes are also useful for adding graphics to a document.

There are also various styles of callout. Text can be added to these shapes to create speech bubbles.

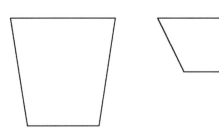

.: Flowcharts :.

Autoshapes can be used to draw flowcharts. The set shapes that fit in with the conventional system for labelling flow charts can be selected.

PC MASTER TIP

Autoshapes can be used to draw stars and banners. You can change the points on a star or change the angle of a banner by clicking on the coloured handles.

01001001010110100101001011101010101011101010110111000001010

 ## SKILL IN ACTION

Sophie the Student uses autoshapes to highlight important parts of her work. She sometimes uses them instead of bullet points to draw attention to areas she will need to revise.

> This is really vital, all essays will probably relate to this!

She can use the shapes to put key points together when planning an essay.

Piggy

He stood for stability. When Piggy went, chaos started.

Ralph

He was the elected leader. He believed the most important thing was to be rescued. Challenged by Jack.

Sophie uses autoshapes to create flowcharts so that she can plan what she is doing.

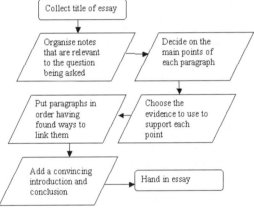

EXERCISE

Can you put a semi-transparent coloured circle over some text to highlight it?

01001010110100101001011101001010101011101010110111000010101 10

SKILLS

.: Autoshapes :.

There are many uses for autoshapes. They can be used as a drawing tool to provide the basic starting points for vector graphics. They can be used to highlight an area of text by applying a colour and making it transparent. They can also be used to label objects or to create logos.

.: Using autoshapes :.

To highlight an area of text, open the Drawing toolbar: click on **View**, **Toolbars** and then select **Drawing**. Click on **AutoShapes** and a menu appears.

.: Using autoshapes :.

Look at the options and select the shape you require. Click where you want it and drag it over the required area. To colour the shape, go to the shape properties, select the colour and make it transparent.

ride in an amusement park. The
see how to collect evidence
get the maximum marks. There
king for when they come to mark

.: Drawing a callout :.

Callouts are also useful for labelling objects. There are many types of callout. Select one from the AutoShapes menu and draw it where you want it to go. To move the pointer, click on the yellow handle and drag it to where you want it. You can then add your text. (See page 50.)

PC MASTER TIP

Autoshapes are also used for labelling work. Add text to a callout and you can point exactly to the area you are commenting on.

PROGRESS CHECK EXERCISE

Can you highlight a paragraph on a page so that it stands out?

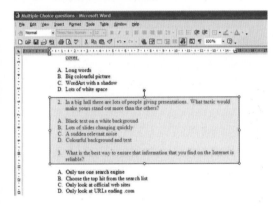

Can you draw a picture of a computer using autoshapes?

To do this, you will need to use 3D shapes or squares.

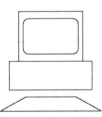

Can you use callouts to make a cartoon?

Make sure that the callout points to the correct part of the image so that it is clear who is talking.

Can you design a logo for a company using autoshapes?

Try to make it as complex as possible, but still look great.

MASTERCLASS

Can you adapt the autoshapes to look a particular way? Try to change the angle of slope or the number of points on a shape. Can you make a face smile or frown?

SKILLS

.: Adding text :.

Sometimes you need to add text to an image. This is very simple whether you are using vector graphics or image applications. It can be useful for adding a logo to an image or for labelling parts of a diagram. You can also add text to make speech bubbles for cartoon characters.

This image of a lorry would look great with a logo on the side.

.: Using autoshapes :.

You can add some text to this cartoon character by using a callout autoshape.

.: Adding text :.

By adding a top layer of text, the lorry can be branded really easily.

PC MASTER TIP

You can add text to any autoshape, but some are already set up as text boxes. Be careful to select the text box tool and not the rectangle tool. Otherwise a cursor will not appear in the box automatically.

0100100101011010010101001011101001010101011010101101100001010

 ## SKILL IN ACTION

Sandy the Secretary sometimes adds text to autoshapes. She thinks that it looks more appealing if the text is highlighted this way and that it stands out more clearly.

In the company newsletter, some pages have articles in autoshapes to make them look more interesting.

Xmas
Party
On Wed
20th

HAPPY
BIRTHDAY
TO RACHEL
IN
ACCOUNTS
21 – (again)

She also occasionally uses this when producing advertising material for the company. It draws the reader's eye to the text and will make the reader see this first.

EXERCISE

Can you make a birthday card with the text in an autoshape?

ONLY
£29.99

1100101010110100101001011101001010101011101010110111000010101101

SKILLS

.: **Adding text to an autoshape** :.

There are two ways to do this. The slower method is to draw the shape and select it so that you can see the handles.

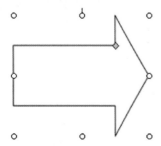

.: **Adding text to an autoshape** :.

While the image is selected, click on **Text Box**, then click inside the arrow. The cursor will appear and you can write the text.

This way to
Rachel's party

.: **Adding text to an autoshape** :.

The quicker way is to use the right mouse click. Select the required shape, then right click on it to bring up a menu.

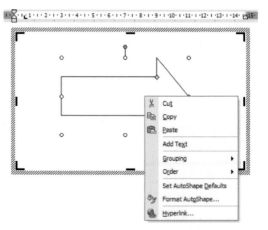

	Cut
	Copy
	Paste
	Add Text
	Grouping ▶
	Order ▶
	Set AutoShape Defaults
	Format AutoShape...
	Hyperlink...

.: **Adding text to an autoshape** :.

Click on **Add Text** and the cursor will appear. You may need to change the size of the font to fit the text in to the shape, or you could change the size of the shape.

💡 PC MASTER TIP

Using the same method it is also possible to add images to an autoshape.

01001001010101101010010100101011101001010101011101010110111000010101

PROGRESS CHECK EXERCISE

Can you add text to a circle to make a road sign?

30

Do this using both ways of adding text to the circle and see which method you find easier.

Can you add text to an arrow to make a direction sign?

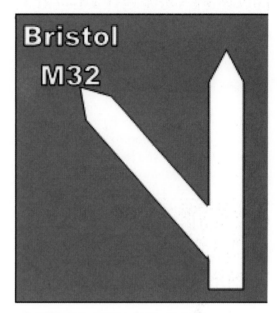

✓ MASTERCLASS

Can you design some hazard signs for your kitchen by using different autoshapes and adding text to them?

SKILLS

.: Flowcharts :.

A flowchart is a very simple diagram that explains what a system does at each stage of a process and what decisions have to be made. Flowcharts are designed to help you follow a process through and to show up bugs (programming errors) in the system. There are programs designed to help you to draw flowcharts. A good example is 'Flowol', but if you do not have this software, you can still draw flowcharts using autoshapes.

.: Flowchart shapes :.

Flowcharts have certain shapes that mean specific things. A list of shapes, with their meanings is shown on the right.

 **Start** or **Stop**

 **Process**

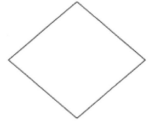 **Decision**

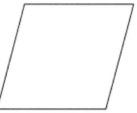 **Input** or **output**

 PC MASTER TIP

It is important that you use the correct shapes for a flowchart, to avoid being misunderstood. If you are not sure what the shapes mean, look them up!

010010010101101001010010101101001010101010111010101011011100001010

SKILL IN ACTION

Donald the Doctor uses flowcharts when checking through procedures that he needs to follow. This helps him to make sure that he covers all possible options when he sees a patient.

The flowchart below is part of one that he uses to make his first diagnosis.

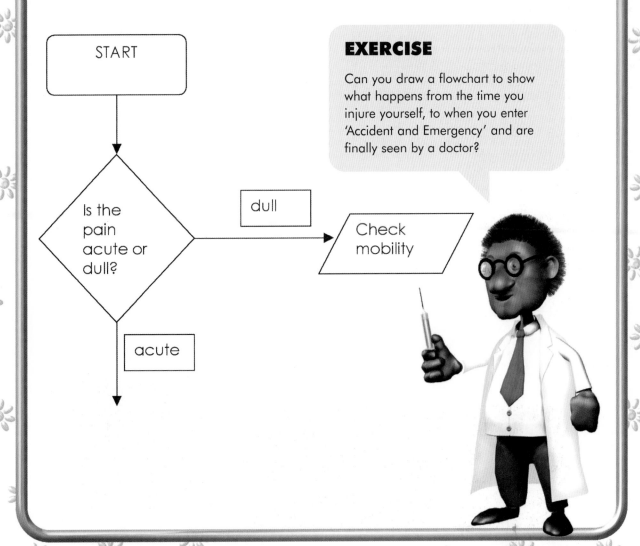

START

Is the pain acute or dull?

dull

acute

Check mobility

EXERCISE

Can you draw a flowchart to show what happens from the time you injure yourself, to when you enter 'Accident and Emergency' and are finally seen by a doctor?

SKILLS

.: Flowcharts :.

Flowcharts have to cover all possibilities. Some software programs only allow you to add the correct number of lines to each box and you can 'run' the flowchart to check that it makes sense. In Microsoft® Word the flowchart symbols are in the AutoShapes menu on the Drawing toolbar.

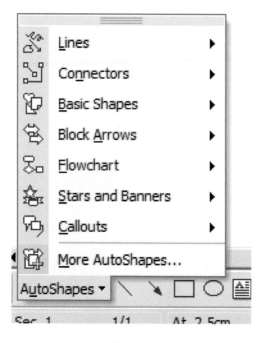

.: Drawing flowcharts :.

Click on **Flowchart** and the flowchart shapes become available.

.: Drawing flowcharts :.

Select the shape you want. Draw where you want it to go and then add text by right clicking on the box. To link the box to another one, use the line tool on the Drawing toolbar or use an arrow. You can then draw the next shape.

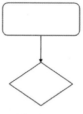

💡 PC MASTER TIP

Every option in a flowchart must lead somewhere. Most boxes have one line in and one line out. There are exceptions though! The start box has no line in and the stop box has no line out. Decision boxes have one line in and two or more lines out, one for each 'answer' to the decision.

PROGRESS CHECK EXERCISE

Can you draw each of the common flowchart shapes and write in the box what each of them is used for?

An example is shown below:

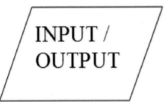

Can you find out what the other symbols on the flowchart mean?

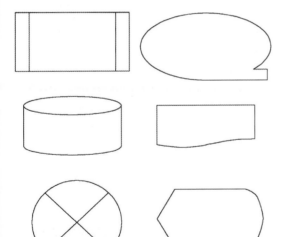

Can you draw a simple flowchart to explain how to make a cup of tea?

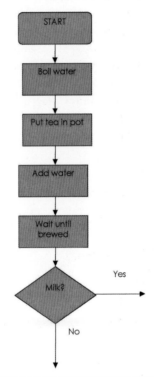

 ## MASTERCLASS

Can you make a flowchart to explain how a system works that flashes lights saying 'slow down', when sensing an approaching vehicle is travelling too fast?

HINT: The speed is the input. The lights are outputs.

FILL AND EFFECTS

SKILLS

.: The fill effects tool :.

Colouring an autoshape is very simple. You have probably used the fill command before. The **fill effects** tool is useful if you need an eye catching document as it allows you to pick a colour that is not the same throughout.

.: Gradient effect :.

You can use a gradient to fade the colour from darker to lighter. This can make your work look more attractive and professional. If you are drawing an object, it will look more realistic as the gradient can be used for shading to give shape.

.: Pattern effect :.

You can select a pattern.

.: Image effect :.

You can select an image.

PC MASTER TIP

The fill effects tool can be used whenever you add a colour using the fill command. Try writing your name in WordArt then adding a photo of yourself as a background. You can find WordArt on the drawing toolbar in Microsoft® Office applications.

0100100101011010010100101011101001010101011101010101101110000101 0

 ## SKILL IN ACTION

Ahmed the Artist uses fill effects to create a background for some of his artwork. He does not like the white background so he either paints the whole canvas a different colour first, or on a computer selects a different colour. The computer has the added benefit of being able to use different colours to make a regular pattern.

He can either have a subtle shade as a background

or he can use some bold colours.

These give a completely different feel to his work and he feels that it gives him the opportunity to express himself in a way that he could not before.

EXERCISE

Can you design a good background for a painting? Use fill effects and think what kind of painting would look good over it.

01001010110100101010010101110100101010101110101010110111000010101110

SKILLS

.: Fill effects :.

This is similar to filling a shape with colour but rather than selecting a colour, you need to click on **Fill Effects**. This is found on the Drawing toolbar by clicking on the small arrow next to the fill button.

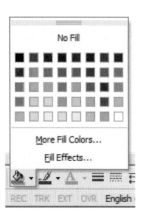

.: The fill effects menu :.

By clicking on **Fill Effects**, the following menu appears:

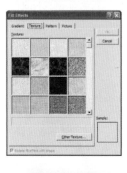

.: The fill effects menu :.

You can select a gradient of colour, where one colour fades into another, or a texture so that the object looks as if it is made of a material, or you could choose a pattern or a picture.

.: The gradient tool :.

One option is to blend two colours together using the **gradient** tool. Some are preset and you can select these in the preset menu, but if you want to choose your own, select the two colours on the **Gradient** menu and then choose how to blend them together using the options below the colour choice.

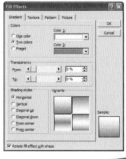

PC MASTER TIP

Most image programs have some kind of gradient function, but they are not always obvious. If you are not sure how to find it, search for 'gradient' on the Help menu.

PROGRESS CHECK EXERCISE

Can you create your own background for a PowerPoint presentation by using fill effects?

Create a background with a pattern.

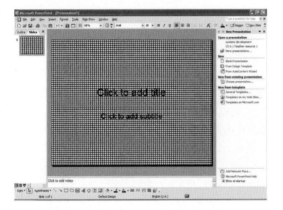

Can you create a box that has a diagonal gradient blending blue and red, blue in the top left and red in the bottom right?

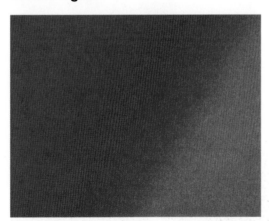

Can you draw a 2D house using textures to make the house look as realistic as possible?

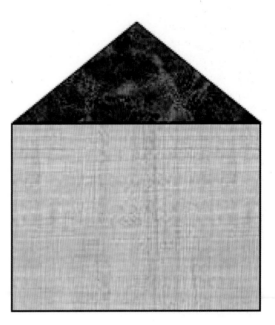

 ## MASTERCLASS

Can you use one of your own photos as a background for a PowerPoint presentation? It is better to fade the image first so that it does not stand out so much that it detracts from the presentation.

CROPPING

SKILLS

.: Cropping :.

It is useful to be able to crop an image because sometimes you need to remove part of the image. One example of where this could be used is when you have taken a photograph and left your finger over the corner of the lens. You can select the part of the photograph that looks best, and crop it so that the rest of the photograph is deleted.

.: Cropping :.

It is also a useful tool if you want to look at one detail of a photograph. You can select this detail and crop it. When you enlarge the photo you will not be wasting memory or ink by keeping the unwanted part of the image.

PC MASTER TIP

You do not have to crop a square or rectangular area, you can select any shape first before cropping by using the lasso tool.

SKILL IN ACTION

Nick the Newspaper Editor uses crop when he has chosen the photographs that will appear in his newspaper. He is given a large selection of images by the photographer and he decides which photograph contains the best detail to complement the story. Once he has the image on computer, he can crop it to select the area that he wants to appear in the newspaper.

The following photograph was taken to illustrate a story about a rescued cat.

Nick decided that the garden was irrelevant to the story. He wanted to zoom in on the cat's face. This gives a much better result as the cat can clearly be seen by the reader.

Nick finds this is especially useful when using photographs of celebrities because they are often photographed from a distance.

EXERCISE

Can you crop a full length image of yourself so that it becomes a head shot?

0100101011010010100101011010010101010111010101101110000010101 10

SKILLS

.: The crop button :.

Cropping is a frequently used tool so it is available in almost all imaging programs. There is sometimes an icon to crop the image.

 Crop icon

.: The crop button :.

Occasionally you need to use the **Crop** command from the toolbar. In Photoshop, this is in the **Image** drop down menu on the main menu bar. However you crop the image, the principle is the same.

.: Making a selection :.

Select the area you want to keep, using the arrow pointer.

Arrow pointer

.: Cropping the image :.

A flashing border will appear around the area and when you are happy with your selection, click on **Crop** on the toolbar or the **crop** icon and the unwanted area will be deleted from the image.

💡 PC MASTER TIP

Be careful! If you save the new image under the same name, the unwanted area is permenantly deleted unless you have kept a backup copy of the original image.

0100100101011010010100101011010010101010110101011011100001010

 PROGRESS CHECK EXERCISE

Can you select a detail from a photograph and crop the image on the computer to change the central point of the photograph?

This is useful when the main object in the photograph is off-centre.

Can you crop a piece of art you have scanned in to select a detail to make into a birthday card?

Crop an image so that the area you are keeping is not a rectangle.

 MASTERCLASS

Crop an image so that it becomes a circle or an oval. The image shape is still a rectangle, but the surrounding areas are transparent. Can you use this image in other programs and keep the transparent area from turning white when you move it?

0100101010110100101001011101001010101011101010110110000101011O

SKILLS

.: The lasso tool :.

This tool is used to select information that you want to delete or copy to another layer or document. There are three types of lasso. Each is useful and should be used at different times.

.: The basic lasso tool :.

The basic lasso tool is the hardest to use because wherever you move the mouse, the selection line will move. It is particularly difficult to use with a laptop, when you are using the touch pad, as it is hard to control where the pointer goes. It is very useful if you want to select a small and irregular area.

.: The polygonal lasso tool :.

When selecting a larger area, the polygonal lasso is the best choice as you have to click to start the selection line and click to end it. Using straight lines makes it very quick to select an area.

.: The magnetic lasso tool :.

Finally, if you want to select a specific object and the colours between the object and those surrounding it are sufficiently different, the magnetic lasso is extremely useful. It follows the border of the object so that you can select it easily.

💡 PC MASTER TIP

It is not always necessary to select an area precisely, you can always delete unwanted parts of an image later. Consider whether it is necessary to spend a lot of time selecting the shape. Could it be done quicker and therefore more efficiently?

SKILL IN ACTION

Nick the Newspaper Editor uses the lasso tool if he has a photograph of a person that he wants, but the surroundings are not appropriate. It is also useful if he just wants a headshot.

He might want to use a photograph of someone's house without giving away the location. The lasso enables him to select the house but delete street signs and neighbours' houses.

He could also take a photograph of someone and use this tool to change the background so that they appear to be somewhere else. He should only do this for fun though!

The three people in the foreground have been superimposed on the photograph so it looks as if they are all in Mauritius.

EXERCISE

Can you download an image from the internet of a location you would like to go to and add yourself to the photograph? You will need to use the lasso tool to select an image of yourself.

010100101011010010100101110100101010101101010110111000010101

SKILLS

.: Using the lasso tools :.

First decide whether you are going to select the area you need or the area you want to remove. It is easier to select the smaller area first. You can always invert the selection by clicking on **Edit** on the main menu bar and then **Invert Selection**.

Next, decide which lasso is the most appropriate for the task.

Right click on the **lasso** button. This gives you a list of lasso options available.

 Lasso Tool

Polygonal Lasso Tool

Magnetic Lasso Tool

.: Selecting with a lasso :.

If you decide to use the basic lasso tool, click where you want to start the selection and carefully guide the pointer along the border of the area you want to select. It can be difficult to select straight lines.

When you are back at the start of your selection, release the mouse.

.: The magnetic lasso :.

If you want to select a specific object, use the magnetic lasso. This is easier to use but there is still a knack to it. Click where you want to start the selection and slowly move around the shape. If the line goes off in the wrong direction, go back to where it was last correct and click the mouse. This fixes the point and you can then click wherever you want to fix further points until the computer finds a clearer colour change in the border again.

.: Deselecting :.

When you have made the selection, it will appear with a dotted line bordering it. If you are not happy with it, you can start again by clicking on **Select** on the main toolbar and then **Deselect**. This might also be under a command **Select None**, or something similar.

PC MASTER TIP

It is better to zoom in as far as you can before using the lasso tool so that you can clearly see what you are selecting.

100100101010110100101001010110100101010101101010110110000101001

 ## PROGRESS CHECK EXERCISE

Can you use the basic lasso tool to select an irregular shaped area and copy and paste it into a word processor?

Can you use the selection tool to select an area of landscape from a photograph to put on a layer for later use to make a background for a presentation?

You will need to crop the image and copy and paste it into Photoshop.

A Presentation about Winchester

Can you use the magnetic lasso tool to select an image of a person or a pet and place them in an unreal situation by altering the background?

 ## MASTERCLASS

Can you take a photograph and break it up into layers by selecting each object in turn and pasting it on to a separate layer?

01001010110100101001011101001010101011101010110111000010101011

SKILLS

.: Layering :.

Layering is used in many of the more advanced image manipulation applications. It is similar to using **Order** in vector graphics but is much more versatile. It is possible to have an image made up of many layers with a different object on each layer. This allows you to edit each object individually without altering any other.

.: Using layers :.

If you are using an image that needs adapting, you can select different parts of the image using the lasso tool then copy and paste each part of the image on to a different layer. You can then work on them separately.

.: The layer menu :.

There is normally a menu that allows you to see what is on each layer. The menu on Adobe Photoshop is shown below.

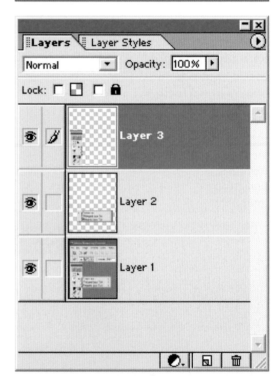

 PC MASTER TIP

The more layers you use to break up the image, the easier it will be to work on just one part of the image without changing the other parts.

SKILL IN ACTION

Max the Marketing Executive uses layering to produce adverts. He can keep the object being advertised in one layer and have different layers for each background he wants. He can then select a background for the object by turning the layers on and off.

Max wants to choose the most appropriate background for the bike. He can place it in the desert:

or by turning that background off and another on, he can set it in the mountains …

… or anywhere.

This makes Max's job easier. He can prepare a number of options for his clients and quickly show them all using his drawing package.

EXERCISE

Set up four or five backgrounds on different layers and add an image on a top layer. Click through the backgrounds and decide which one looks the best.

SKILLS

.: Using layers :.

It is important to plan what you want to do with an image before you start creating it in a program that uses layers. Decide what needs to be on each layer so that you can save time if you decide to manipulate the image later. Practise using the layering system by drawing a rectangle with a plain background. Use the airbrush tool to add a second colour and a bit of texture to the background.

.: Using layers :.

Now create a second layer by clicking on the **New Layer** button. On the second layer, fill the rectangle in completely with a third colour. The first two colours will disappear under the new colour. Now use the **eraser** tool to draw a pattern or write a word. The layer below will become visible.

.: The eye button :.

You can turn the layers on and off by selecting the **eye** icon on the Layers menu.

 Eye icon

💡 PC MASTER TIP

If you are trying to manipulate an image and it is not working, check which layer you are on. It is easy to get it wrong!

0100100101011010010100101011010010101011010101011011000101011

 ## PROGRESS CHECK EXERCISE

Can you create a new layer?

Can you change the head on a person by having pictures of two people on different layers?

Erase all of the image on the top layer except the head. The head should now be floating around the image on the lower layer. You can move it and resize it so that it fits perfectly over the head of the first person.

 ## MASTERCLASS

Can you make yourself look like a professional sportsperson by adding your head to an image of them in action?

010010101011010010101001010110101010101101010101101110000101010

SKILLS

.: The pipette tool :.

The pipette tool is very useful when you are manipulating images. It is used to colour match objects. If you are manipulating an image or if you are trying to touch it up to improve it, it is often very hard to choose a colour identical to the one required.

.: The pipette tool :.

The pipette tool can select a colour from part of the image rather than from the colour palette. This means that the added brush strokes will be indistinguishable from the original work.

Adobe Photoshop

File   Edit   Image   Layer   Select   Filte

Sample Size: Point Sample

192.psd @ 100% (Laye

.: Using the pipette tool :.

The photograph above is in the process of being improved. The pipette is used to select the nearest colour to the fold and the brush fills in the white fold. The pipette needs to be used regularly during this process as the colour changes as you move from one area to the next.

 PC MASTER TIP

The pipette is usually used on an image that has been taken with a digital camera, scanned in or copied from the internet. You could also use it to match a colour you have made by blending layers together. These colours could be blended by using an airbrush, different styles of brush or the opacity tool.

SKILL IN ACTION

Tammy the Teacher uses the pipette tool to touch up photos that she is using to make worksheets. She often scans pages from magazines and uses the images. Occasionally, the image is across the fold in the magazine or has staples going through it. She gets rid of any marks left by colouring over them with the brush tool. It is important that the colour is right so she uses the pipette to select the colour.

The image below is going to be used on a worksheet about British wildlife, but Tammy wants to improve the quality first. To avoid copyright problems, Tammy needs to contact the magazine to check she can use the image.

She works on it until the fold is invisible.

EXERCISE

Can you use the pipette to select the colour from a picture so that you can improve a photograph using that colour?

SKILLS

.: Using the pipette tool :.

It is very simple to select a colour using the pipette tool. It is what you do with the colour that is the skill. The pipette tool is normally accessed using a button on the Toolbox toolbar or the Graphics toolbar.

 Pipette tool

.: Using the pipette tool :.

Click on the **pipette** tool and the cursor changes to a pipette. Find the colour on your image that you want to use, click on it and the colour box will change to your chosen colour.

You can now select the **paintbrush** tool and paint with this colour.

 Paintbrush tool

Colour Palette

.: Using the pipette tool :.

This poster was made with as close a colour match as possible.

Using the pipette it is easy to give the text exactly the same colours as the flashes.

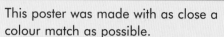

PC MASTER TIP

If you are replacing a thin line with colour, you will need to select the colour at almost every point using a pipette, as the colour will probably change slightly as you move across the image.

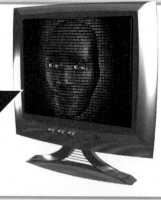

PROGRESS CHECK EXERCISE

Draw two circles. Colour one circle in using a colour from the custom palette.

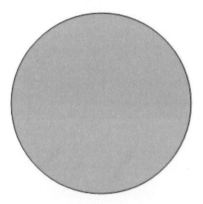 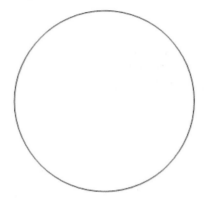

Using the pipette tool, can you colour the second circle in exactly the same colour?

Can you repair a photograph by matching the colours carefully as you work across the image?

 ## MASTERCLASS

Can you blend skin tones on a head that has been superimposed on to a different body by selecting the colours from either the face or the body using the **pipette** tool?

01001010101101001010100101011101001010101011101010110110110000101010

SKILLS

.: Brush size and pressure :.

It is possible to alter how the brush makes its mark on the page by changing the brush options. You can make the brush thicker or thinner, make a solid mark as if the brush was thick or a finer mark as if the brush had fewer, finer bristles. This can create an interesting effect if you do not want the colour to be consistent throughout. The finer colour around the edge gives a soft focus effect.

.: Brush pressure :.

You can also change the opacity of the line. This means that you can change the pressure exerted by the brush so that, by applying lighter pressure, it does not completely cover up the layer below.

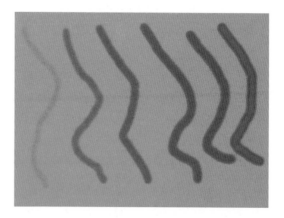

.: Brush pressure :.

By increasing the pressure, the lines become more opaque as they move to the right.

PC MASTER TIP

Experiment with different brushes for different effects. Do not be afraid to try a new style of brush.

01001001010110100101010010101101010101101011100001010

SKILL IN ACTION

Ahmed the Artist changes the brush size when creating images on the computer in the same way that he would when using a paintbrush on canvas. The larger the brush, the faster he covers an area. The smaller the brush the finer the detail he can draw. He changes the style of the brush, in the same way that he would with real paint, to alter the effect of the final piece of work. He achieves a more textured finish by using a brush with fewer, finer bristles. The background below has been painted using this method. Notice how you can see the individual brush strokes.

When you compare this with the same rectangle coloured in using a solid brush, it is clear that the effect is very different.

This gives Ahmed a more authentic background as if he had painted it by hand. The image below does not look as though it was created with a brush.

EXERCISE

Can you colour two rectangles in using two different types of brush? Which do you think makes a better background?

BRUST SIZE AND PRESSURE

SKILLS

.: Brush size and style :.

Changing the brush size and style is easy and uses the same method. To see the different types of brush available there is a menu that can be accessed by clicking on the arrow next to the brush size button on the toolbar.

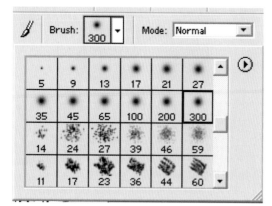

.: Brush style :.

There are other types of coverage to choose from. This is all you need to be able to change the size and style of brush from a thick line to a thin line.

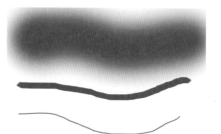

.: Opacity :.

To change the opacity, you need to look at the pressure 'slider' when the brush tool is selected. 100% opacity will not allow any of the lower layer to be seen through. 1% will only fade it very slightly.

PC MASTER TIP

By changing the opacity you can highlight an area of a photograph. You can do this by putting a coloured box in a layer on top of the area to be highlighted. Make the opacity about 50% and use the eraser tool. This will erase 50% of the colour so that you can see through it.

PROGRESS CHECK EXERCISE

Can you change the style of the brush to draw a thick, solid line?

Now draw a thin line.

Change the brush tool so that the line is thick but textured.

Fill in the background layer with a solid colour.

Can you draw a line that fades as you move across from one side of the image to the other?

Try this by decreasing the pressure. Compare this to using an airbrush and moving it faster or slower.

 MASTERCLASS

Can you produce a soft focus edge around a photo using the brush tools to blend the image in with its surroundings?

COLOUR BALANCE

01001010110100101001011101000101010101011101010110111000010101

SKILLS

.: Colour balance :.

Colour balance is the way in which the colours compare to one another. In some of the better image applications, e.g. Adobe Photoshop, you can vary the degree of each colour in the image. In other applications this option is restricted to the brightness and the amount of red, blue and green.

.: Colour balance :.

Once you have your image in the program, colour balance can be used to restore the original colour, improve the quality of the photograph or produce a zany effect. There is an option in the edit toolbar in Adobe Photoshop called variations. This shows you what the image will look like if the colour is altered slightly.

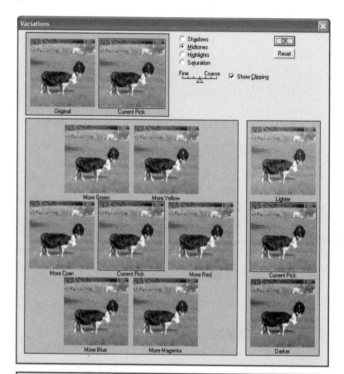

.: Colour balance :.

You can change the colour more dramatically by looking at the colour graphs produced and adapting them. The best way to learn how to use these is by trial and error as there is so much that they can do.

 PC MASTER TIP

Remember that there is always an Undo option if you do not like the effect.

01001001010110100101001011101001010101011101010101101110000101 0

SKILL IN ACTION

Harry the Hotelier uses colour balance to enhance digital photos that he takes to put on the hotel website. He believes that if the photographs look a bit brighter they will make the weather appear better, which might make his hotel look more appealing to stay at than some others.

The following photograph was taken in October.

He also uses the same functions to improve photographs taken indoors at events that he wants to publicise.

By brightening the image and adding a bit more yellow, the weather looks much better.

EXERCISE

Can you select the sky on an image and brighten it to make it look sunnier?

`1001010110100101001011101001010101011101010110111000010101101`

SKILLS

.: The colour balance tools :.

There are three basic tools for altering the colour of an image and many more advanced tools. The simplest alteration to make is to change the brightness and the contrast. This is done by clicking on **Enhance** on the main menu bar and then **Brightness and Contrast** on the drop down menu.

.: The brightness/contrast tool :.

In the image of the eagle below, the second section has had the brightness increased, and the third section has had the contrast increased.

.: The colour variation tool :.

Using variations is a simple way of slightly altering the colour. First click on **Enhance**, then click on **Variations**. You can choose from a selection. You can then apply it and save it. Repeat the process if necessary.

.: The hue and saturation tool :.

The third method is to alter the colours yourself. This is done by altering the hue and saturation. To open the menu, click on **Enhance**, then **Colour** and finally **Hue and Saturation**. Drag the slider bars, to see how the image changes. This tool can make dramatic changes.

PC MASTER TIP

With any of these methods, only the area selected will be altered, the rest of the image will stay the same, so you can change the background without changing the foreground.

01001001010110100101001011101001010101110101011011100001010

 # PROGRESS CHECK EXERCISE

Draw a red oval. See how you can change the colour by using variations.

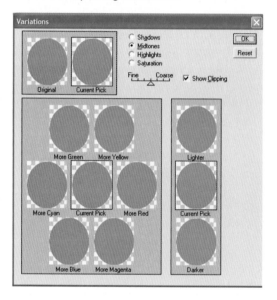

Draw the red oval again. This time look at what happens when you brighten the oval.

Using what you have learned from these two tasks, can you change the weather on a photograph by brightening up the sky?

HINT: If you are still having problems, try the same functions with blue and green ovals.

 ## MASTERCLASS

Find an old photograph that has faded or yellowed. Can you restore this to its original colours by changing the colour balance?

SKILLS

.: Dodge and burn :.

These two tools are really the opposite of each other. They are both used to alter imperfect photographs. If a photograph is too dark, you can use the dodge tool. You can select whatever brush size you want and move the brush over the image. This will brighten the areas that you pass over. It will not work for a totally black photograph.

.: The dodge tool :.

Using the dodge tool, the photograph looks much better and is worth printing out.

.: The burn tool :.

The burn tool is the opposite of the dodge tool. If the photograph has caught the sun and is too bright, the burn tool can restore it as long as the image is not completely white.

 PC MASTER TIP

These tools can also be used to add highlights and lowlights to images that you are creating.

SKILL IN ACTION

Nick the Newspaper Editor uses these tools to touch up photographs for his newspaper.

Sometimes the photographer takes a perfect picture, but the photo is too dark or too bright. Sometimes a colour photograph needs to be printed in black and white. It may lack contrast so Nick can choose to add highlights and lowlights to improve it.

The photo below will be fine in colour, but may look too pale in black and white.

The improved photograph will look much better when printed.

EXERCISE

Can you change a photograph from colour to black and white? Now alter the photograph so that it is clearer.

SKILLS

.: The dodge and burn tools :.

As the dodge and burn tools are rarely used at the same time, they are both options on the same button. If one is showing and you want to use the other button, you need to right click on it. These buttons are found on the toolbox menu.

.: The burn tool :.

The burn tool will make the area you pass the brush over darker.

 Burn tool

.: The dodge tool :.

The dodge tool will make the area you pass the brush over lighter.

.: Dodge and burn :.

The image below has a stripe that was done using the dodge tool on the left and the burn tool on the right.

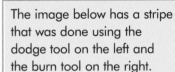 **PC MASTER TIP**

To brighten a large area, it is better to use a very large brush (you can select a large custom size – try 300). A small brush may leave streaks across the image and the brightening will be less consistent.

01001001010101101001010010101101001010010101101010110111000010101

PROGRESS CHECK EXERCISE

Can you add shading to a solid filled circle to make it look like a 3D sphere?

You will need to use the **dodge** tool to brighten an area and make it look like a reflection of light.

You can use the **burn** tool to create a darker area in the shade.

Can you darken the sky on a photograph to make it look more dramatic?

The image below has a red swipe drawn across it made by using the brush tool. This is faded to give an evening sunset feel.

Can you improve a dark photograph taken indoors to make it look brighter?

✔ MASTERCLASS

Can you improve the appearance of the weather in a photograph to make it look as though the photo was taken on a sunny day?

SKILLS

.: The clone tool :.

This is a useful tool for image manipulation. You can select an area of a photograph and then click where you want it copied. As you move the brush over the area, the application copies the image from where you clicked originally.

.: Using the clone tool :.

This is best explained with an example. The image below was photographed but it was felt that there was too much concrete.

.: Using the clone tool :.

To give more of a 'wildlife' feel to the area, the flowers can be copied to cover the concrete. By using the clone tool, the following image can be produced:

.: Multiple images :.

This tool can also be used for making two heads and producing multiple images. It saves having to use the pipette to copy large areas of colour where there is a slight change as you move along.

 PC MASTER TIP

This is a useful tool but you need to be careful how far you move without clicking on a new area. You might start copying parts of the image that you do not want if you are too far from the original point.

SKILL IN ACTION

Max the Marketing Executive uses the clone tool to improve the backgrounds for some of the products he advertises. A photograph might have a building on it that he does not want or it may contain objects which would draw attention away from the product being advertised.

The landscape below would be great except for the fact that the extra buildings rather spoil the image. By clicking below the unwanted buildings and cloning the trees, Max can copy over the unwanted buildings. This is a quick way of manipulating an image without having to crop it.

EXERCISE

Can you clone a photograph of your garden so that it looks as if it is one big lawn? This will make a better background for photographs of people as attention will not be drawn to the borders.

Without the buildings, the landscape looks much better. Max needs to touch it up a bit using other tools before it is finished.

0100101010110100101001011101001010101011101010110111000010101 10

SKILLS

.: The clone tool :.

Cloning an image is a skill worth practising. Remember that the first place in which you hold down the **Alt** button and click the cursor, is the first place that will be copied when you next click the cursor. Before you click on the clone tool you should make sure that both areas are on the screen so that you can clearly see what you are copying and where you are cloning it to. The clone button is on the toolbox along with the brush tools.

 Clone tool

.: Selecting an image :.

The pointer will change shape; you now need to click on the area that you are going to clone. In the case of the next image, it will be an area of grass.

.: Cloning an image :.

Once you have selected the area to be cloned, you can start covering the area you want to replace. Click in the centre of this area and hold the mouse button down as you move around. In this case, the area will be covered in grass.

PC MASTER TIP

If you start getting areas that you do not want to clone because you are moving too far from the original point, start the process again and you can clone as before.

1001001010110100101001011101001010101101010110111000010101

 PROGRESS CHECK EXERCISE

Can you clone part of an image to remove an unwanted area?

Look at the picture of the football stand. To make the ground look fuller, clone the crowd from one area to copy it over the blank seats.

It now looks much more impressive.

Can you give yourself a second head using the clone tool?

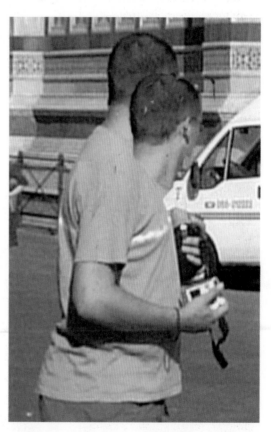

 MASTERCLASS

Can you make a photograph of your garden look more impressive by cloning the best parts to make the borders look full of flowers?

RESIZING PART OF THE IMAGE

SKILLS

.: The resize tool :.

The resizing tool is useful when you are combining two layers to make one image. The images may be different sizes and the proportions would look wrong if you stuck one head on another body, or a house might look far too big in a landscape.

.: The resize tool :.

By resizing the head you can correct it so that it looks in proportion to the rest of the photograph.

.: Using the resize tool :.

The footballers have been superimposed on the background of an empty pitch. They look too big for the stadium but once they have been resized, the photograph looks more genuine.

PC MASTER TIP

Resizing part of the image can only happen with objects in different layers. It is therefore better to plan to use two different layers when you open or copy the images.

SKILL IN ACTION

Vicrum the Vet offers a service where he can superimpose a photo of his customers' pets into locations that the family have been to, so that it appears as though the pet went on the trip. His greatest problem is that the images that he has of the pets are far too big compared to the photographs of the family on holiday.

The cat is too close up.

Once the images have been combined and resized, the effect is very good.

EXERCISE

Can you resize a photograph of a pet so that it looks smaller compared to its background?

SKILLS

.: Resizing part of an image :.

To resize the image of the footballers from the previous page, copy a photograph of a stadium into the background and the footballers photograph into a second layer. Select the footballers only and delete the rest of the second layer. This will leave you with some large footballers on a background. Click on **Image** on the main menu bar and then **Resize** and finally **Scale**.

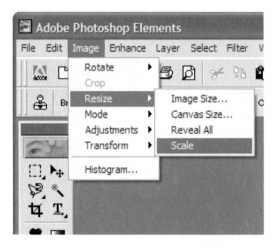

.: Resizing part of an image :.

Click on the centre of the area selected to move the image in relation to the background or click on the corners to resize the image. Once you are happy with the image you can combine the layers and the photograph is complete.

PC MASTER TIP

Remember that the images need to be on different layers. If they are not you can lasso them to select an object and copy them on to a different layer. Then you can start working with them.

PROGRESS CHECK EXERCISE

Draw a rectangular background.

Can you draw a series of circles decreasing in size, by copying and pasting circles onto different layers and resizing each circle?

Draw a small circle on one layer and a larger irregular shaped object on the next.

Can you use the resize tool to fit the irregular shaped object inside the circle?

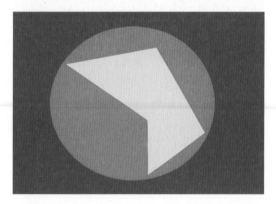

 MASTERCLASS

Use the **lasso, delete** and **layer** tools to produce an image of a head on a different body. Can you resize the head to fit on the body?

INDEX